MEL BAY PRESENTS

SONGS OF FRANCE

(Chansons Françaises)

By Jerry Silverman

D1500958

Contents

NI Introduction

This traditional street cry of the itinerant song seller is the best way I can think of to introduce the collection of *chansons françaises*. For just as the peddler had in his sack of broadsides for every taste, here, too will hopefully be found a pleasing potpourri of ballads, songs and snatches—singing of soldiers and sailors, lovers false and true, working people and people who never did an honest day's work in their lives, priests and revolutionaries, and even a song in praise of the guitar!

Those of you who will sing these songs in French will come across some "misspelled" words or "ungrammatical" sentences in a few of the songs. These are not typographical errors, but are traditional (folksy, if you like) variants commonly found in folk songs of France, and other lands as well.

With that warning out of way, there are only two more words that need be said here:
Chantons! - Let's sing!

Voi - là, L'mar-chand d'chan-sons qui pas - se, Voi - là. L'mar-chand d'chan
Here's the sel - ler of songs who's pass - ing, Here's the sel - ler of

sons;_____ De bell's chan-sons pour ceux___ qui___ les ai - ment, De
songs;_____ Of beau-ti - ful songs for those___ who___ do love them, Of

bell's chan-sons pour ceux qui les chan-te - ront.____ Voi - là, L'mar-chand d'chan-sons qui
beau-ti - ful songs for those___ who-will sing them.____ Here's the sel - ler of songs who's

pas - se, Voi - là l'mar-chand d'chan-sons._____
pass - ing, Here's the sel - ler of songs._____

De tous côtés que je me tourne
Each Way I Turn

French soldiers' songs are among the most widely known songs of "occupations." Here, a young recruit bound for the Napoleonic campaign in Russia, has a bitter leave-taking with his "true love" - who, it turns out, has given him nothing but trouble.

De tous côtés que je me tourne, Je sens mon coeur embarrassé.
Each way I turn it doesn't matter, I feel my heart is full of

sé. Ma mère m'a cherché misère, Ma maîtress' m'a délaissé.
pain. My mother only brings me sorrow, I'll not see my love again.

sé. Et moi dans la promptitude, J'ai parti pour m'engager, Et moi
gain. So I quickly as I could then, Joined the army right away, So I

dans la promptitude, J'ai parti pour m'engager.
quickly as I could then, Joined the army right away.

M'y promenant dedans la ville,
Ma maîtresse j'ai rencontré.
Et partant avec ma maitresse
Ma maîtress' s'met à pleurer.
Je lui ai demandé: - Belle,
Qu'avez-vous à pleurer?   ) 2

- On dit partout dedans la ville
Que vous vous êtes engagé.
-Celui qui t'a dit ça, la belle,
T'a bien dit la vérité,
Car j'ai trois campagn's à faire
Et mes amours à délaisser.   ) 2

- Quand tu seras dans la Russie
Ah! récris-moi ton arrivée!!
Si tu as fait z'un bon voyage,
Et si tu es en bonn' santé.
Si tu as fait z'un bon voyage,
Et si tu pens's à m'épouser.   ) 2

-A t'épouser, dis-tu, ma belle?
A moi z'il ne faut plus penser.
Tu as trop fait la difficile.
Partout tu m'as méprisé.
Maintenant c'est à mon tour.
Adieu, la belle, c'est pour toujours.   )2

As I did walk about the city,
My true love I did chance to spy.
And when I parted from my true love,
She began to weep and cry.
I then asked her: "Tell me, darling,
You are weeping - tell me why?"   ) 2

"People say all throughout the city,
That you have joined the army, dear."
"Those who have told you that, my darling,
Have all said the truth, I fear.
For I've three campaigns to go through,
While my love I do leave here."   ) 2

"And when you find yourself in Russia,
Write just as soon as you arrive.
If you did have a pleasant voyage;
I must know if you're alive.
If you've had a pleasant voyage,
And you want me for your bride."   ) 2

"Marry you, do you say, my darling?
You must no longer think of me.
You always have been so contrary,
You have scorned me bitterly.
Now it is my turn to leave you;
Fare thee well - it's for always!"   ) 2

De terre en terre
From Earth to Earth

The wine grower in his vinyard has always appeared in poetic imagery as the model *par excellence* of the happy man. This traditional song from the Champagne region is a perfect example of the genre. It is sometimes entitled *Le cycle du vin* ("The Cycle of Wine") for reasons that will become apparent in singing it.

De terre en terre,
La voilà la jolie terre,
Terri ter-rons ter-rons le vin,
La voilà, la jolie terre au vin,
La voilà, la jolie ter-re.

From earth to earth,
Here it is the pretty earth now,
The earth, The earth the earth, the vine,
Here it is, the pretty earth for wine,
Here it is, the pretty, earth now.

De terre en plante,
La voilà la jolie plante,
   Planti, plantons,
   Plantons le vin,
La voilà la jolie terre au vin,
La voilà, la jolie terre.

From earth to plant,
Here it is, the pretty plant now,
   Let's plant, let's plant,
   Let's plant the vine,
Here it is, the pretty earth, for wine,
Here it is the pretty earth now.

Similarly

De plante en pousse...	From plant to bud...
De pousse en branche...	From bud to branch...
De branche en feuille...	From branch to leaf...
De feuille en fleur...	From leaf to flower...
De fleur en graine...	From flower to seed...
De graine en mûre...	From seed to fruit...
De mûre en grappe...	From fruit to bunch...
De grappe en cueille...	From bunch to pick...
De cueille en cuve...	From pick to vat...
De cuve en foule...	From vat to crush...
De foule en presse...	From crush to press...
De presse en tonne...	From press to cask...
De tonne en perce...	From cask to pierce...
De perce en broc...	From pierce to jug...
De broc en verre...	From jug to glass...
De verre en goûte...	From glass to taste...
De goûte en trinque...	From taste to toast...
De trinque en bouche...	From toast to mouth...
De bouche en ventre...	From mouth to gut...
De ventre en terre...	From gut to earth...
De terre en plante...	From earth to plant...

Le hareng saur
The Salted Herring

This lively dance comes from the fisherfolk of Flanders who ply the colder waters in search of the fish that is called "the king of the sea." Its totemistic quality is reminiscent of many songs of outdoor occupations, where the worker-singers' livelihood (and often, life) depends on the caprices of nature.

C'est en l'hon-neur du ha - reng saur que l'on chan - te, Et
In hon - or of the salt - ed her - ring we sing our song, Be -

sa tê - te d'a - bord il faut que l'on van - te. Pre -
cause its head is the first thing that we bring a - long. Get

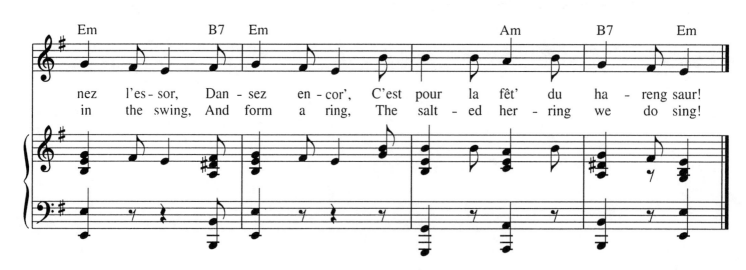

nez l'es - sor, Dan - sez en - cor', C'est pour la fêt' du ha - reng saur!
in the swing, And form a ring, The salt - ed her - ring we do sing!

C'est en l'honneur du hareng saur que l'on saute,
Il a l'œil plus voyant que le garde-côte:
   Prenez l'essor,
   Sautez encor',
C'est pour l'œil du hsreng saur.

Jeunes fillett's, trémoussez-vous à la danse,
Du hareng saur la mer réfléchit la panse;
   Prenez l'essor,
   Dansez encor'
C'est pour la pans' du hareng saur.

C'est par la queu' du hareng que je termine,
Elle est plus blanch' que celle de la Dauphine;
   Prenez l'essor,
   Sautez encor',
C'est pour la queu' du hareng saur.

In honor of the salted herring we jump around,
A sharper eye than his just never can be found.
   Get in the swing,
   And form a ring,
The herring's eye is why we sing.

Young girls, why don't you move about and join the dance?
The salted herring's belly reflects the sea's expanse.
   Get in the swing,
   And join the ring,
The herring's belly is why we sing,

It's by the herring's tail that I do end my song.
It's whiter than the dolphin's, and I am not wrong.
   Get in the swing,
   And from a ring,
The herring's tail is why we sing.

HARENG SAUR

(FLANDRE)

C'est en l'honneur du hareng saur que l'on chante,
Et sa tête d'abord il faut que l'on vante;
   Prenez l'essor,
   Dansez encor,
C'est pour la têt' du hareng saur.

Braves mineurs
Brave Miners

Miners, like sailors, are very superstitious. They consider it very dangerous to sing or even whistle while working. The offended Spirit of the Mine would invariably be provoked into releasing an escape of that terrible and deadly fire damp gas that smells of freshly peeled potatoes, and which explodes when mixed with air. Perhaps this is the reason why this song is one of the very few French miners' songs.

Bra - ves mi - neurs, Puis - que nous somm's en - sem - ble,
Min - ers so brave, Be - cause we are to - geth - er,

Oh - é - oh! oh - é - oh! Il faut nous di - ver - tir! Dans ces ro - chers, Nous
Oh - ay - oh! oh - ay - oh! We must a - muse our - selves. We are ex - posed a -

somm - es ex - po - sés. Mal - gré le dan - ger, Il nous faut tra - vail - ler!
mong the fall - ing rocks. Spite of all the dan - ger we all have to work!

Mais quand nous somm's de cinq cents pieds en terre,	But when we are five hundred feet below ground,
Nous ne craignons ni grêle ni tonnerre.	We fear not hail nor thunder's mighty roar.
Souvent la pluie	Often the rain
Nous cause de l'ennui.	Does trouble us a bit.
Tout ça n'fait pas peur	But none of this does scare
A ces braves mineurs.	The brave miners so rare.
Lorsque je suis dans un si beau fonçage,	When I am in the bottom of the pit,
Ah! que le temps il me devient charmant	Ah! how the time becomes so pleasant.
Près d'un' maîtresse	Close to a girl
Qu'elle est jolie et belle.	Who's beautiful to see.
Ça fait du bonheur	That's the best of times
A ces braves mineurs.	For these brave miners.
Quand j'ai chargé mon charmant coup de mine,	And when I load my charming blasting charge,
Et que la poudre est prête à éclater,	And when the powder is ready to explode,
Par un' cannette	With a quick shot
Qui est toujours prête,	That always is red hot,
Dans un peu de temps,	In no time at all,
Il y a du changement.	There are some changes made.
J'ai parcouru les puissanc's étrangères,	I've travelled throughout many foreign countries,
Mais c'est toujours la France la plus belle.	But France is always the most pretty.
Mineur de houille,	Miner of coal,
Mineur de plâtre aussi,	Miner of plaster too,
Dans ce département	In this department
On le sait bien choisi.	We know well which to chose.
Si vous connaissez le directeur des mines,	If you do know the director of the mines,
Oui, c'est un brave et bon enfant	Yes, he's a worthy and a good guy.
Quand il voit venir	And when he sees
Tous ses mineurs charmants.	All his charming miners drawing near,
Mais cela lui fait plaisir	It gives him the greatest joy
De leur compter d'l'argent.	To count out their money.
Qu'est-ce qu'a composé c't'aimable chansonnette?	And who composed this pleasant little song?
C'est trois mineurs de renom et pas bêtes,	Three well-known miners who're no fools.
En venant de Blanzy	Arriving from Blanzy,
Pour venir au Creusot	And coming to Creusot,
Tenant sur ses genoux,	Holding on their knees
La plus bell' d'ses amies.	The prettiest of girls.

Quand Marion s'en va-t-à l'ou
When Marion Goes to the Pond

This is one of those songs whose humor lies in folksy mispronunciation (in French) of the rhyming words of each verse. The *"l'ou"* in the title is a variant of *"l'eau"* (water). A number of the other *"ou"* words are similar distortions.

Quand Ma-ri - on s'en va-t-à l'ou, Quand Ma-ri-
When Ma-ri - on goes to the pon(d), When Ma-ri-

on s'en va-t-à l'ou, Ne mar-che pas, mais court tou - jou. Dé-ri - rou,
on goes to the pon(d), She does-n't walk she'd rath-er run.

bah, bah, bah, dé-ri-ret-te, gai, gai, Oh gai, gai, dé-ri-ret - te.

Ne marche pas, mais court toujou':(2)
Dans son chemin trouve l'amou'. *Chorus*

Dans son chemin trouve l'amou': (2)
"Amou-s-amou, embrassons-nous. *Chorus*

Amou-s-amou, embrassons-nous.(2)
-Faisons vite et dépêchons-nous: *Chorus*

Faisons-vite et dépêchons-nous: (2)
J'ai tant d'ouvrage à la maisou'. *Chorus*

J'ai tant d'ouvrage à la maisou'.: (2)
La pâte est prêt', le feu au fou'. *Chorus*

La pâte est prêt', le feu au fou'; (2)
Et mon mari qu'est un jalou'. *Chorus*

Et mon mari qu'est un jalou'; (2)
Que les jaloux fuss'nt des moutous. *Chorus*

Que les jaloux fuss'nt des moutous; (2)
Et moi la bergère de tous. *Chorus*

Et moi la bergère de tous: (2)
Je les ferais manger au loup. *Chorus*

She doesn't walk, she'd rather run, (2)
And on the way she finds her hon'. *Chorus*

And on the way she finds her hon', (2)
"O, lovey-dove, let's have some fun! *Chorus*

"O, lovey-dove, let's have some fun!(2)
Let's do it quick, and hurry on." *Chorus*

"Let's do it quick, and hurry on, (2)
There's work at home that must be done." *Chorus*

"There's work at home that must be done, (2)
It's time the baking was begun." *Chorus*

"It's time the baking was begun, (2)
My husband is a jealous one." *Chorus*

"My husband is a jealous one; (2)
Would jealous men did sheep become." *Chorus*

"Would jealous men did sheep become, (2)
And I were shepherdess - what fun!" *Chorus*

"And I were shepherdess - what fun! (2)
The wolf would eat them - every one!" *Chorus*

N'allez pas au bois, Jeanne
Don't Go to the Woods, Jeanne

This song from Gascony is all about wild beasts and apples... or is it?

N'al - lez pas au _____ bois Jean - ne,
"Don't _____ go to the _____ woods, Jean - ne,

N'al - lez pas au _____ bois, Jean -
Don't _____ go to the _____ woods, Jean -

ne, Seu - let - te, Sans _____ ber - ger.
ne, All _____ a - lone, With - out a shep - herd."

Il y a un' bêt' sauvage, (2)
Peut-êt' vous mangerait.

- S'avez peur qu'ell' me mange, (2)
V'nez avec moi garder.

- T'jours j'vais avec vous, belle, (2)
Jamais rien n'me donnez.

- Que voulez - vous qu' j'vous donne? (2)
J' n'ai rien à vous donner.

- Donn' moi vos pommes, belle. (2)
- Mûr's elles ne sont pas.

- Et quand ell's seront mûres? (2)
- Pierre, vous les aurez.

Les pomm's, et aussi l'arbre, (2)
Tout ce que vous voudrez.

"There is a wild beast yonder, (2)
Maybe it will eat you."

"If you fear it will eat me, (2)
Come and protect me."

"I always go with you, my pretty, (2)
You never give me anything."

"What do you want me to give you? (2)
I have nothing to give you."

"Give me your apples, my pretty." (2)
"They are not ripe yet."

"And when they will be ripe?" (2)
"Pierre, you shall have them."

"The apples and also the tree; (2)
Everything that you want."

15

Le premier jour de novembre
The First Day of November

One of the subjects dearest to the popular French soul in general, and the Breton soul in particular, is the tale of the poor girl who, against all odds, is able to keep her "honor". The story of Marivonik and the Saxon king, Gradlon, was sung by itinerant ballad singers who entertained fairgoers in Brittany. These singers (*ménétriers*) hardly exist any more, but from the 15th century until the reign of Louis XIV (in the 18th century) they constituted a powerful guild. No one could join the guild without the consent of their "king". They played the *bombarde* (a double reed instrument) and the bagpipe. A true *ménétrier* was recognized by the grace notes with which he delighted in decorating his melodies—never playing the same song quite the same way twice.

Dourdu (actually, Dourduff) is a river valley in northern Finistère.

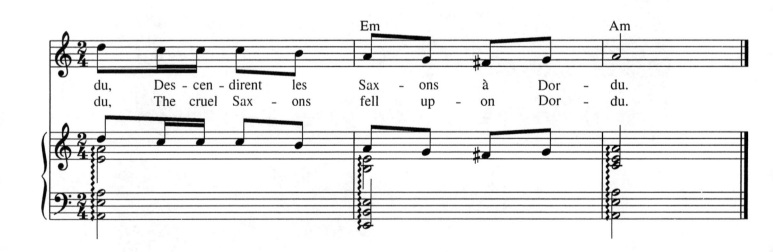

A Dourdu sont descendus.
Ils ont volé une jeune fille. (2)

Ils ont volé une jeune fille.
Pour l'emmener dessus leur bâtiment. (2)

- Adieu, mère, adieu, mon père,
Jamais ne me reverrez en ce monde. (2)

A Marivonik a dit
Le capitaine quand il vit cela: (2)

- Votre vi' n'la perdrez pas.
Pour votre honneur, je ne vous dis pas non. (2)

- M'sieu le capitain', dit's–moi:
A combien d'entre vous serai livrée? (2)

- A moi, à mon valet d'chambre,
A mes mat'lots quand ils auront envie. (2)

Mes mat'lots sont cent et sept."
Marivonik se jeta dans la mer. (2)

Un petit poisson blanc l'avale,
Et la rend à la porte de son père. (2)

- C'est votre fille qui demande l'entrée
Après avoir conservé son honneur."(2)

They descended on Dourdu,
And they captured a young girl.(2)

Yes, they captured a young girl,
For to transport her to their great ship. (2)

"Farewell, mama - farewell, papa,
You'll not see me again in this world." (2)

To Marivonik then did say
The captain when he saw all this: (2)

"Your sweet life you will not lose,
But as for your honor, I can't say." (2)

"O, tell me, captain, I would know,
To how many of you will I go?" (2)

"To me and to my serving man,
And to my crew when they feel like it." (2)

"One hundred seven men have I."
Marivonik then leaped into the sea. (2)

A little white fish swallowed her,
And brought her to her father's door. (2)

"Your daughter wishes to come in,
And with her honor still intact." (2)

Le garçon jardinier
The Gardener Lad

Gardeners were members of a tightly controlled guild, like harvesters, with whom they had close relationships; they married only among each other. However, what might happen "on the mountain, beneath the mulberry tree," was nobody's business.

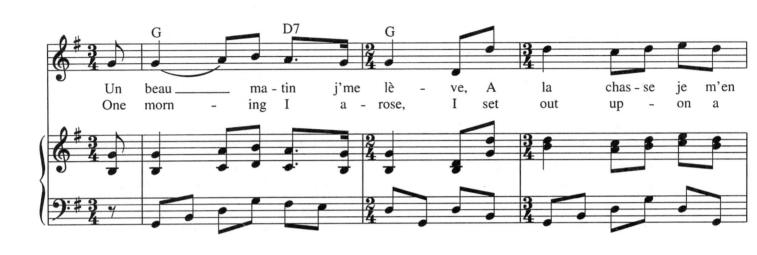

Un beau _____ ma - tin j'me lè - ve, A la chas - se je m'en
One morn - ing I a - rose, I set out up - on a

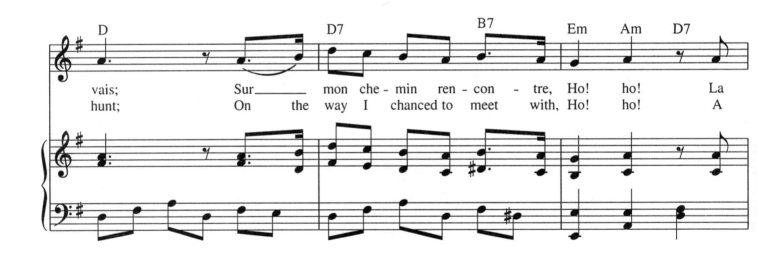

vais; Sur _____ mon che - min ren - con - tre, Ho! ho! La
hunt; On the way I chanced to meet with, Ho! ho! A

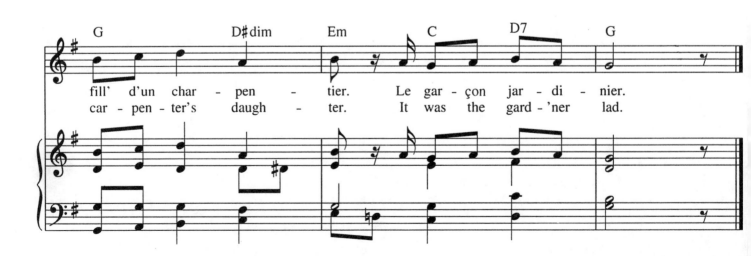

fill' d'un char - pen - tier. Le gar - çon jar - di - nier.
car - pen - ter's daugh - ter. It was the gard -'ner lad.

-Où allez-vous, la belle,
Où allez-vous si matin?
- Je m'en vais à la messe
    Ho! ho!
V's entendez bien sonner,
Le garçon jardinier.

- Il est trop matin, la belle;
Venez donc dans mon jardin.
Je la prends par sa main blanche.
    Ho! ho!
Au jardin l'ai menée,
Le garçon jardinier.

- Oh! choisissez, la belle,
La fleur que vous voudrez.
Mais tout en cueillant la rose,
    Ho! ho!
Ell' se mit à pleurer,
Le garçon jardinier.

-Quoi pleurez-vous, la belle?
De quoi vous chagrinez?
- Je pleur' mon coeur en gage
    Ho! ho!
Car je l'ai bien donné
Au garçon jardinier.

- Pleurez pas tant, la belle,
Car je vous le rendrai
La-haut sur la montagne,
    Ho! ho!
A l'ombre d'un mûrier,
Le garçon jardinier.

"Where are you bound, my pretty?
So early in the morn?"
"I'm going off to mass now,
    Ho! ho!
Hear the church bells in the air.
    It was the gard'ner lad.

"My dear, it is too early,
So come into my garden."
And I took her by her white hand,
    Ho! ho!
To the garden I led her.
    It was the gard'ner lad.

"O, you may choose, my pretty,
The flower that you desire."
But as she did pluck the rose,
    Ho! ho!
A tear came to her eye.
    It was the gard'ner lad.

"Why do you cry, my pretty,
What is troubling you?"
"Because my heart is pledged,
    Ho! ho!
I've given it away,
    All to the gard'ner lad."

"Don't cry so much, my pretty,
For I'll give it back to you,
Way up there on the mountain,
    Ho! ho!
Beneath the mulberry tree."
    It was the gardner lad.

Les trois princesses
The Three Princesses

Der - rièr' chez mon pè - re,
Near my fa - ther's dwell - ing,

Vo - le, vo - le, mon coeur, vo - le,   Y'a un pom - mier doux.   Tout
Fly, O, Fly a - way my dear heart,   There's an ap - ple tree.   You

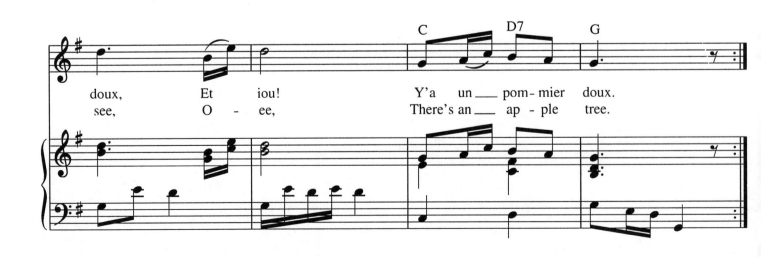

doux,   Et iou!   Y'a un __ pom - mier doux.
see,   O - ee,   There's an __ ap - ple tree.

Trois belles princesses,
Vole, vole, mon coeur, vole,
Sont couchées dessous!
Tout doux, et iou!
Sont couchées dessous.

Çà, dit la première,
Vole, vole, mon coeur, vole,
Je crois qu'il fait jou'!
Tout doux, et jou!
Je crois qu'il fait jou'!

Çà, dit la seconde,
Vole, vole, mon coeur, vole,
J'entends le tambou'!
Tout doux, et iou!
J'entends le tambou'!

Çà, dit la troisième,
Vole, vole, mon coeur, vole,
C'est mon ami doux!
Tout doux, et iou!
C'est mon ami doux.

Il va-t-à la guerre,
Vole, vole, mon coeur, vole,
Combattre pour nous!
Tout doux, et iou!
Combattre pour nous.

S'il gagne bataille,
Vole, vole, mon coeur, vole,
Aura mes amou's!
Tout doux et iou!
Aura mes amou's.

Qu'il perde ou qu'il gagne,
Vole, vole, mon coeur, vole,
Les aura toujou's!
Tout doux, et iou!
Les aura toujou's.

Resting 'neath its branches,
Fly, o fly away, my dear heart,
Are princesses three.
You see, o - ee.
Are princesses three.

O, then says the first one,
Fly, o fly away, my dear heart,
It's dawning o'er the lea.
You see, o - ee.
It's dawning o'er the lea.

O, then says the second,
Fly, o fly away, my dear heart,
I hear drummery.
You see, o - ee.
I hear drummery.

O, then says the third one,
Fly, o fly away, my dear heart,
It is my sweetie.
You see, o - ee.
It is my sweetie.

He is off to battle,
Fly, o fly away, my dear heart,
Fighting for us three.
You see, o - ee.
Fighting for us three.

If he wins the battle,
Fly, o fly away, my dear heart,
He'll have all of me.
You see, o - ee.
He'll have all of me.

If he wins or loses,
Fly, o fly away, my dear heart,
I will constant be.
You see, o - ee.
I will constant be.

LES TROIS PRINCESSES

I

Derrièr' chez mon père,
Vole, vole, mon cœur, vole,
Y a un pommier doux !
Tout doux, et iou !
Y'a un pommier doux.

Pâtre montagnard
Mountain Shepherd

Collected by composer Vincent D'Indy in the Vivarais region (the eastern border of the *Massif Central,* between the Loire and the Rhône).

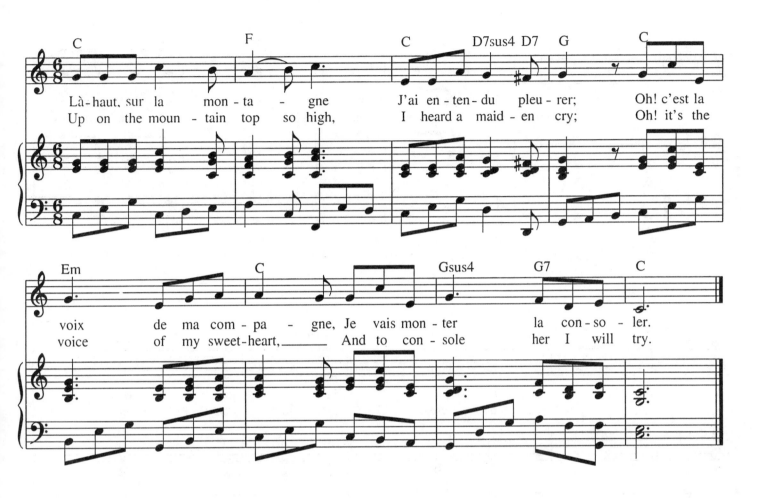

- Et qu'avez - vous, la belle,
Qu'avez - vous à pleurer?
Oh! si je pleur', c'est de tendresse,
Et de regret d'avoir aimé.

D'aimer n'est pas un crime,
Dieu ne le défend pas.
Faudrait avoir l'âme bien dure
Si ces deux coeurs ne s'aimaient pas.

Les moutons sont en plaine,
En grand danger du loup,
Tandis que vous et moi, bergère,
Sommes après faire l'amour.

Les moutons vivent d'herbe,
Les papillons de fleurs,
Et vous et moi, jeune bergère,
Nous ne vivons que de l'amour.

"And what's the matter, sweetheart,
Tell me why do you cry?"
"Oh, if I cry, it's tenderness,
And of regret of having loved."

Loving is certainly no crime,
God does not frown on it.
You'd have to have a hardened soul,
For these two hearts never to love.

The flock of sheep is on the plain,
A dangerous wolf nearby.
While you and I, my shepherdess,
Know true love's sweet tenderness.

All of the sheep, they live on grass,
Butterflies live on flowers.
But you and I, my sweet young girl,
We live by this love of ours.

Père capucin
Capuchin Father

A Capuchin friar belongs to the branch of the Franciscan order that observes vows of poverty and austerity. They are the subject of many humorous, and often lascivious, songs. This one just hints at things to come.

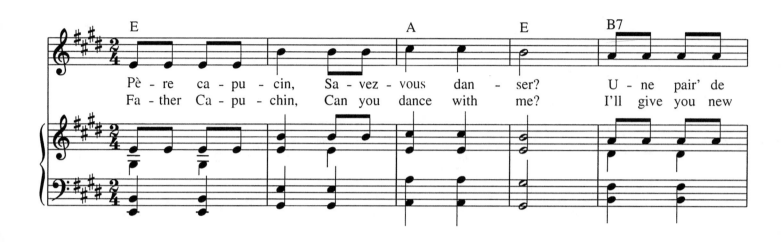

Pè - re ca - pu - cin, Sa - vez - vous dan - ser? U - ne pair' de
Fa - ther Ca - pu - chin, Can you dance with me? I'll give you new

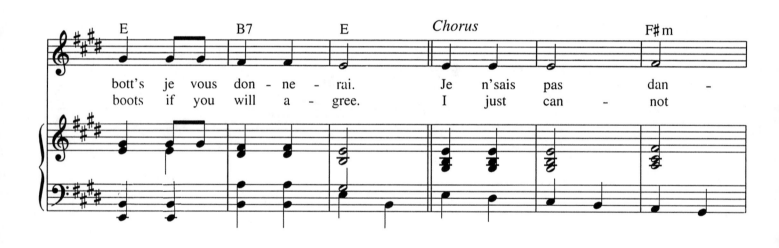

bott's je vous don - ne - rai. Je n'sais pas dan -
boots if you will a - gree. I just can - not

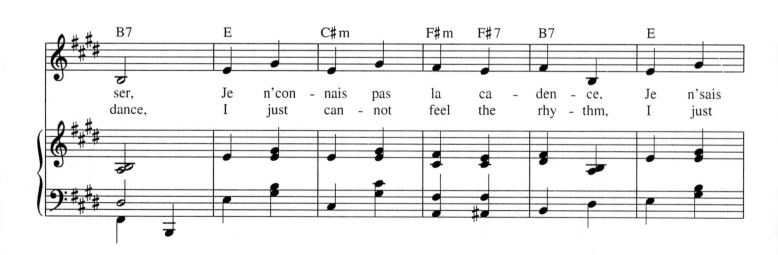

ser, Je n'con - nais pas la ca - den - ce, Je n'sais
dance, I just can - not feel the rhy - thm, I just

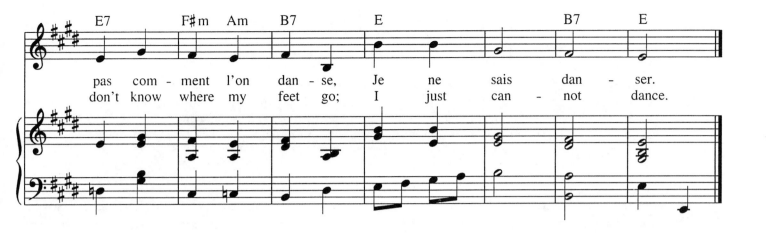

Père capucin, savez-vous danser?	Father Capuchin, can you dance with me?
Un manteau de bur' je vous **donnerai**. *Chorus*	I'll give you a cloak if you do agree. *Chorus*
- Père capucin, savez-vous danser?	Father Capuchin, can you dance with me?
Un beau capuchon je vous donnerai. *Chorus*	I'll give you a hood if you do agree. *Chorus*
- Père capucin, savez-vous danser?	Father Capuchin, can you dance with me?
Un beau chapeau rond je vous donnerai. *Chorus*	I'll give you a hat if you do agree. *Chorus*
- Père capucin, savez-vous danser?	Father Capuchin, can you dance with me?
Un chap'let d'argent je vous donnerai. *Chorus*	A silver rosary if you do agree. *Chorus*

La joile fille de La Garde
The Pretty Maiden of La Garde

Another song in which the modest maiden would rather die than suffer "a fate worse than death" — in this case, with a surprise ending. The story line in this ballad is somewhat unclear: Just who kidnaps the girl—the duke? the captain? or some unnamed third party? The song seems to be hoping the captain gets there on time—but from where? And who is the duke anyway? *Hélas!* we shall never know.

La Garde is in southern France not far from Toulon.

Au châ - teau — de La Garde, Il y'a trois bel-les fil - les, Au châ-
In the cha-teau of La Garde, There are three pret-ty maid - ens, In the

teau — de La Garde, Il y'a trois bel-les fil - les.
cha-teau of La Garde, There are three pret-ty maid - ens.

Il y'en a un' plus bel - le que le jour; Hâ -
And there is one who's pret - tier than the day; Make

te - toi, ca-pi - tai - ne, Le duc va l'é - pou-ser.
hoste, Brave cap-tain, hur - ry, The duke will mar - ry her.

En dedans son jardin,
Suivi de tout' sa troupe,
En dedans son jardin,
Suivi de tout' sa troupe,
Entre et la prend sur son bon cheval gris,
Et la conduit en croupe
Tout droit en son logis.

Aussitôt arrivé',
L'hôtesse la regarde:
Aussitôt arrivé',
L'hôtesse la regarde:
"Et's - vous ici par force ou par plaisir?
-Au château de La Garde
Trois cavaliers m'ont pris."

Dessus ce propos-là.
Le souper se prépare,
Dessus ce propos-là.
Le souper se prépare:
"Soupez, la bell', soupez en appétit"
Hâte - toi, capitaine,
Voici venir la nuit.

Quand l'souper fut fini,
La belle tombe morte,
Quand l'souper fut fini,
La belle tombe morte,
Ell' tombe morte pour plus ne r'venir:
Au jardin de son père
Il nous faut revenir.

"Sus, mes bons cavaliers,
Sonnez de vos trompettes,
Sus, mes bons cavaliers,
Sonnez de vos trompettes;
Ma mie est mort', sonnez piteusement:
Nous allons dans la terre
La porter tristement.

- De nos fols ennemis
N'est-ce pas l'avant-garde?
De nos fols ennemis
N'est-ce pas l'avant-garde?
Baissez la hers', et nous nous défendrons:
Cette tour, Dieu la garde!
Point ils ne la prendront.

-Beau Sire de La Gard',
Ouvrez-nous votre porte,
Beau sire de La Gard',
Ouvrez-nous votre porte,seconde,
Vot' fille est mort', là-bas dns le vallon;
Un serpent l'a mordue
Dessous son blanc talon.

And within her garden walls,
Followed by her troop was she.
And within her garden walls,
Followed by her troop was she.
He comes in and carries her away,
Behind him on his steed,
To his dwelling straightaway.

The hostess looked at her,
Soon as she entered the yard.
The hostess looked at her,
Soon as she entered the yard.
"Have you come here by force or by free will?"
"At the château of La Garde,
Three knights captured me."

Upon these very words,
The supper was prepared.
Upon these very words,
The supper was prepared.
"Eat well, my dear, and with good appetite."
Captain, quick! Have no fear,
The night will soon be here.

And when supper was all done,
The maiden fell down dead.
And when supper was all done,
The maiden fell down dead.
She fell down dead, and never to return.
To the garden of her father,
We must return again.

"Up, my horsemen, so brave,
And sound your trumpets loud.
Up, my horsemen, so brave,
And sound your trumpets loud.
My love is dead, sound out piteously,
We will take her to the earth
Sadly, wrapped within her shroud."

"Of our crazy enemies,
Isn't that the avant-garde?
Of our crazy enemies,
Isn't that the avant-garde?
Drop the gate, and let's defend ourselves.
This tower, may God save it!
They will never take it."

"Good Lord of La Garde,
Open up your door for us.
Good Lord of La Garde,
Open up your door for us.
Your girl is dead, down there in the valley.
She was bitten by a snake,
Below her white heel"

"Il nous faut l'enterrer
Au jardin de son père,
Il nous faut l'enterrer
Au jardin de son père,
Sous des rosiers tout blancs ct tout fleuris,
Pour mieux conduir' son âme
Tout droit en paradis."

Quand ils fur'nt dans l'jardin,
La belle ressuscite;
Quand ils fur'nt dans l'jardin,
La belle ressuscite;
"Bonjour, mon père, bonjour vous soit donné.
Bonjour, j'ai fait la morte
Pour mon honneur garder."

Et quand les rosiers blancs
Eurent fleures nouvelles,
Et quand les rosiers blancs
Eurent fleures nouvelles:
"Allons, ma fille, il faut vous marier."
Ah! pauvre capitaine,
Le duc va l'epouser!

"Now we have to bury her
In her father's garden green.
"Now we have to bury her
In her father's garden green.
'Neath the roses all white and in flower,
Better to fly her soul
Direct to Paradise."

When they were in the garden,
The maiden she awoke.
When they were in the garden,
The maiden she awoke.
"Good day, my father, I wish you a good day.
My death I did dissemble,
To keep my honor pure."

And when the white roses
Did flower once again.
And when the white roses
Did flower once again.
"Come, come, my girl, it's time to marry you."
O, my poor captain,
The duke will marry her!

Passant par Paris
As Through Paris I Passed

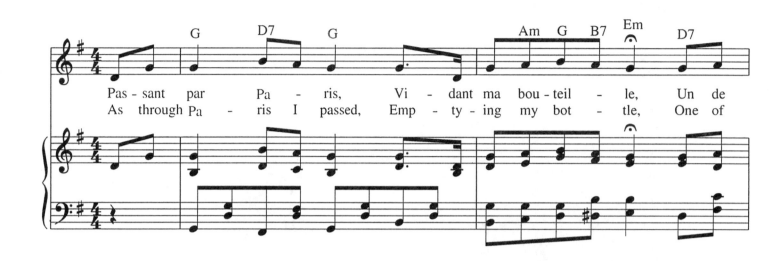

Pas - sant par Pa - ris, Vi - dant ma bou - teil - le, Un de
As through Pa - ris I passed, Emp - ty - ing my bot - tle, One of

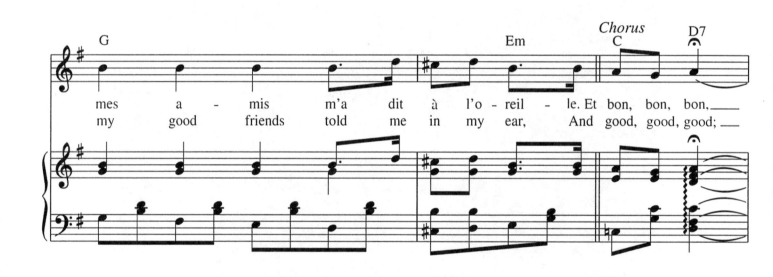

mes a - mis m'a dit à l'o - reil - le. Et bon, bon, bon,____
my good friends told me in my ear, And good, good, good;____

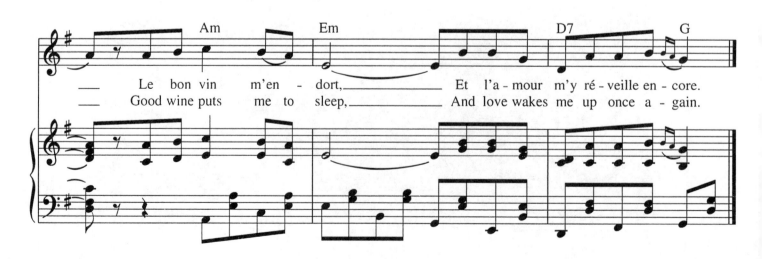

____ Le bon vin m'en - dort,_____ Et l'a - mour m'y ré - veille en - core.
Good wine puts me to sleep,_____ And love wakes me up once a - gain.

Prends bien garde à toi	Take good care of yourself,
Quand tu coupes l'herbe;	When you cut the grass.
Laisse-la couper	Once it is cut,
Reviendra plus belle. *Chorus*	The nicer it comes back. *Chorus*
Les prés ont des fleurs	In the meadows are flowers,
Jaunes et vermeilles.	Yellows and bright reds.
Moi, j'ai dans mon coeur	Me, I have in my heart,
Une fleur dorée. *Chorus*	A golden flower instead. *Chorus*
Fleuris, belle fleur,	You will never have
Ma fleur sans pareille,	What I got from her.
Fleuris dans mon coeur,	I got from her heart
Fleuris pour ma belle. *Chorus*	The prettiest flower. *Chorus*
Tu n'auras jamais	Blossom, pretty flower,
Ce que j'ai eu d'elle.	My unequalled flower.
J'ai eu de son coeur	Blossom in my heart,
La fleur la plus belle. *Chorus*	Blossom for my love. *Chorus*
J'ai couché trois ans	And I slept three years,
La nuit avec elle	Each night next to her,
Dans de beaux draps blancs	Under sheets so white,
Garnis de dentelle. *Chorus*	Covered with fine lace. *Chorus*
Elle a trois enfants	She has children three,
Dont je suis le père.	I am the father,
L'un est à Bordeaux,	One is in Bordeaux,
L'autre à La Rochelle, *Chorus*	The other is in La Rochelle. *Chorus*
L'autre est au pays.	And the third roams 'round,
Il fait comm' son père.	He does like his dad.
Il aim' bien les filles,	He just loves the girls,
Caress' la bouteille. *Chorus*	The bottle makes him glad. *Chorus*

Jean-François de Nantes
Jean-François of Nantes

Boney was a warrior,
Away ah yah!
A warrior and a terrior,
John Franswah.

This English sailors' song about the rise and fall of Napoleon has the same melody as *Jean-François de Nantes.* Just as British and French navies battled each other across the high seas for hundreds of years (or, perhaps, because of it) British and French tars "exchanged" songs - including borrowing from each other's language.

C'est Jean - Fran - çois de Nan - tes, Oué. Oué, Oué. Ga-
It's Jean - Fran - çois of Nan - tes, Way, Way, Way. Top-

bier de *la Frin - gante,* Oh me bouées, Jean - Fran - çois.
man of the *Frin - gante,* Oh me boys, Jean - Fran - çois.

Débarque de campagne
Oué, oué, oué.
Fier comme un roi d'Espagne.
Oh! Mes bouées Jean-François.

Debarked from a campaign,
Way, way, way.
Proud as a king of Spain,
Oh! my boys, Jean-François.

Similarly

En vrac dedans sa bourse
Il a vingt mois de course.

His purse is very heavy,
From twenty months at sea.

Une montre, une chaîne
Qui vaut une baleine.

He has a watch and chain,
The whaleman feels no pain,

Branl'bas chez son hôtesse
Carambole et largesses.

Carousing all the first night,
With presents left and right,

La plus belle servante
L'emmèn' dans sa soupente.

The barmaid with the blonde hair,
Did lead him up the stairs,

De concert avec elle
Navigue sur mer belle.

The two of them together,
Did sail in pleasant weather,

En vidant la bouteille
Tout son or appareille.

But when he had his last drink,
His gold did make a clink,

Montre, chaîn' se balladent.
Jean-François est malade.

So, no more watch and chain,
Jean-François now feels pain.

A l'hôpital de Nantes
Jean-François se lamente.

In hospital in Nantes,
Jean-François does lament.

Et les draps de sa couche
Déchire avec sa bouche.

The sheets upon his bed,
He chews into small shreds,

Pauvr' Jean-François de Nantes
Gabier de *la Fringante*.

Poor Jean-Françcois of Nantes,
Topman of the *Fringante*.

La chanson du rémouleur
The Sharpener's Song

Je suis-t-un fort bon
I am a first - class

ré - mou - leur, Je suis-t-un fort bon ré - mou -
sharp - en - er, I am a first class sharp - en -

leur, Mais pour ma fil - le j'ai grand peur,
er, My girl, what will be - come of her,

Si je la mène sur mon train,
Si je la mène sur mon train,
Cela lui gâtera le teint,
Cela lui gâtera le teint,
Et dans les rues j'ai grand' peur
    Qu'on ne me la...
    Car elle est bien gentille.

Si je la donne au capucin,
Si je la donne au capucin,
Il me la f'ra mourir de faim,
Il me la f'ra mourir de faim,
Pard' sous leur mandrill', j'ai grand' peur
    Qu'on ne me la...
    Car elle est bien gentille.

Si je la donne au cordonnier,
Si je la donne au cordonnier,
Il me la f'ra marcher nu-pieds;
Il me la f'ra marcher nu-pieds,
Dans sa boutique j'ai grand' peur
    Qu'on ne me la...
    Car elle est bien gentille.

Si je la donne au jardinier,
Si je la donne au jardinier,
Il m'la mettra en espalier,
Il m'la mettra en espalier;
Dans l'orangeri' j'ai grand' peur
    Qu'on ne me la...
    Car elle est bien gentille.

Si je l'embarque sur la mer,
Si je l'embarque sur la mer,
Ce sera pour jamais la r'voir,
Ce sera pour jamais la r'voir;
Et dans les îles j'ai grand' peur
    Qu'on ne me la...
    Car elle est bien gentille.

If on my job I take her in,
If on my job I take her in,
That will most surely ruin her skin,
That will most surely ruin her skin.
And in the streets, I am afraid
    That someone will...
    For she is very pretty,

If I give her to a Capuchin,
If I give her to a Capuchin,
She'll surely starve - or at least, get thin,
She'll surely starve - or at least, get thin,
Beneath his cloak, I am afraid
    That someone will...
    For she is very pretty,

If I give her to the shoemaker,
If I give her to the shoemaker,
He'll make her walk with her feet all bare,
He'll make her walk with her feet all bare.
Down in his shop, I am afraid
    That someone will...
    For she is very pretty,

If I give her to the gardener,
If I give her to the gardener.
Onto the trellis he'll hook her,
Onto the trellis he'll hook her.
In his orange grove, I am afraid
    That someone will...
    For she is very pretty,

And if I send her off of sea,
And if I send her off of sea,
That is the last that she'll see of me,
That is the last that she'll see of me.
For in the islands, I am afraid
    That someone will...
    For she is very pretty,

Chanson du cidre
Song of Cider

Normandy is renowned for its apples, cider and *calvados* (a potent applejack, or hard cider). Judging by the Latin invocation of the Deity, it is probably this latter decoction that is being sung of here.

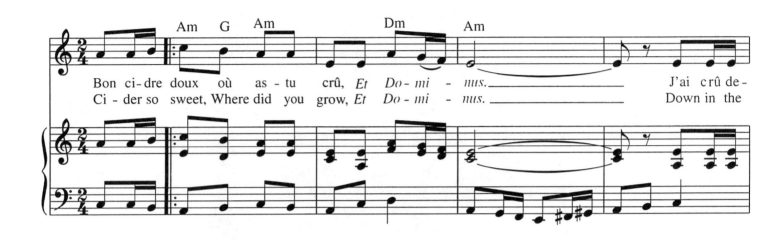

Bon ci-dre doux où as-tu crû, Et Do - mi - nus._____ J'ai crû de-
Ci - der so sweet, Where did you grow, Et Do - mi - nus._____ Down in the

dans ce bois tor - tu. A coups d'gour-dins on m'a bat-tu, Puis en pan-ier l'on m'a fou -
for - est grove be - low. Felled by a cud-gel's heav - y blow, In a bas-ket I was then

tu. As - per - ge me *Do - mi - ne.*_____ Puis en pan - ne._____
thrown. O sprink-le me *Do - mi - ne.*_____ Then in a ne._____

Puis en panier l'on m'a foutu,
Et Dominus.
Dans un banneau l'on m'a chargé.
Jusqu'au pressoir on m'a trainé,
Sur la rou' l'on m'a écrasé.
    Asperge me *Domine.*

Puis sous la roue on m'a moulu,
Et Dominus.
Sur la fesselle on m'a monté.
Dans un' cuve on m'a égoutté,
Dans un' cuve on m'a entonné.
    Asperge me *Domine.*

Then in a basket I was thrown,
Et Dominus.
Then in a hamper I was packed,
Into the press I then was stacked,
And on the wheel I then was cracked.
    Sprinkle me *Domine.*

Under the wheel I then was squeezed,
Et Dominus.
Into the strainer I was poured,
Into a vat I then was low'red,
Then in a barrel I was stored.
    Sprinkle me *Domine.*

39

Gugusse

This song springs from the fiddlers who played at country weddings in the 19th century. The word "polka" first entered the French language in 1842. "Gugusse" is the diminutive of Gustave.

C'est Gu - gusse a - vec son vio - lon_____ qui fait dan - ser les fil - les, Qui
It's Gu - gusse with his vi - o - lin,_____ Who gets the girls a - danc - ing, Who

fait dan - ser les fil - les. C'est Gu - gusse a - vec son vio - lon, Qui fait dan - ser les filles et
gets the girls a - danc - ing, It's Gu - gusse with his vi - o - lin, Who gets the girls to dance; The

les gar - çons. Mon pa - pa ne veut pas que je dan - se, Que je dan - se,
Il di - ra ce qu'il vou - dra, Moi je dan - se, Moi, je dan - se,
boys join in. My pa - pa does-n't want me to dance so, Me to dance, no.
Let him talk, Let him squawk, I'll go danc - ing I'll go danc - ing.

Mon pa - pa   ne veut pas   que je dan - se la pol - ka.
Il di - ra   ce qu'il vou - dra,   Moi je dan - se la pol - ka.
My pa - pa   does - n't like   when I'm danc - ing the pol - ka.
Let him talk,   Let him squawk,   I'll go danc - ing the pol - ka.

41

Les tisserands
The Weavers

The weavers' workshops used to be the grand gathering places of young people of both sexes. Weavers were in the highest ranks of story tellers and ballad singers. The endless repetitive clicking of the loom (*métier*) furnished an ideal rhythmic accompaniment to many a weaver's song. The word *métier* has taken on the wider meaning of trade, craft or profession.

Les tis - se - rands sont pir' que des é - vê - ques. Les tis - se - rands sont pir' que des é - vê - ques. Tous les di - manch's ils en font u - ne fê - te, Bran - lons la na - vet - te. Oh! gai la la. Bran - lons la na - vet - te, Le beau temps re - vien - dra.

The weav - ers are much worse than all the bish - ops. The weav - ers are much worse than all the bish - ops. On each Sun - day they have them - selves a par - ty. Let us shake the shut - tle. O! click, clack, clack, Let us shake the shut - tle, Good times are com - ing back.

substitute "new days' here.

Chorus

42

Each verse starts out with the same lyrics as verse one; then the "new day" is substituted.

Et le lundi, ils vont boir' chopinette. *Chorus*   And on each Monday, they drink a stein of beer. *Chorus*

Et le mardi, ils vont voir leurs maîtresses. *Chorus*   And on each Tuesday, go to see their mistress. *Chorus*

Et l'mercredi, ils vont r'boir' chopinette. *Chorus*   And on each Wednesday, another stein of beer. *Chorus*

Et le jeudi, ils faisont 'leurs couchettes. *Chorus*   And on each Thursday, they go to make their bunks. *Chorus*

Et l'vendredi, commenc'nt leur semaine. *Chorus*   And on each Friday, they all begin their week. *Chorus*

Sing the next 6 lines to measures 9-12 repeated six times before going on to the chorus.

Et le sam'di: - Nous faut de l'argent, maître.   And on each Saturday: "We need some money, boss.

- Tu n'en auras pas qu'la pièc'ne soit faite.   "You won't get a thing until your work is done."

- Fait'z'ou non fait', me faut de l'argent, maître.   "Whether done or not, I need my money, boss.

J'prnds ma navett', j'te la fous par la tête.   I'll take my shuttle and bash it on your head,

Et l'espoulex', je l'fous par la fenétre.   And the cylinder, I'll fling it out the window.

Moi, j'm'en irai boire une chopinette. *Chorus*   I'm gonna have another stein of beer." *Chorus*

43

Le piocheur de terre
The Ditch Digger

Instead of fighting her headstrong daughter, who wants to marry - *Mon Dieu!* - a ditch digger,
mama actually writes a letter to the "contractor", asking him to come up with a worthy candidate.
Of course, it doesn't work out. Maybe the girl will marry that rich farmer after all.

C'est un' jeune fil - le de quinze ans, S'en va dire à sa mè -
It's a young girl, fif - teen years old, Who goes to tell her moth -

re, C'est un' jeune fil - le de quinze ans, S'en va dire à sa mè -
er, It's a young girl, fif - teen years old, Who goes to tell her moth -

re: Ma-man, m'y fau - drait un____ a mant, Je l'ai-me - rai si ten - dre -
er: Ma- ma, I need some-one____ to love, I'd love him, O, so ten - der -

ment, Tout com - me vous aim - iez mon pè - re._____
ly, Just the way you did love my fa - ther._____

44

Oh! va, ma fill', que penses-tu? } 2
    C'est un piocheur de terre!
Nous qui n'avons que toi d'enfant,
Nous te marirons richement;
Tu seras grosse fermière.

O! go, my girl, what's on your mind? } 2
    He's just a lowly ditch digger!
We, who have only you, my child,
We'll find for you a much better match;
You will be a rich farmer's wife.

Grosse fermièr' m'appartient pas, } 2
    Je n'suis pas assez riche;
J'aimerais mieux mon cœur placé
Avec un jeune terrassier,
Quoiqu'il sera piocheur de terre.

Rich farmer's wife is not my style, } 2
    I'm just not rich enough for that.
I would much rather give my heart
To a young man who works the land,
Even if he's a ditch digger.

Eh bien, ma fill', nous écrirons } 2
    L'entrepreneur de route;
Qu'il te choisisse un terrassier,
Pour qu'il soit parfait à ton gré,
Tout le long de la rivière.

Well then, my girl, we'll write a note } 2
    To the contractor of the road;
That he should choose one of his men,
Who would suit you in every way,
All out along the river bank.

L'entrepreneur a répondu } 2
    Une triste nouvelle:
Les chantiers sont finis partout,
Les terrassiers s'en vont tertous;
Adieu donc, belle lingère.

The contractor did answer them, } 2
    With this unhappy news:
The work sites are all finished here,
The diggers scattered everywhere;
Farewell then, pretty seamstress dear.

Qu'en a composé la chanson? } 2
    C'est trois piocheurs de terre;
Etant buvant au cabaret;
La maîtresse les écoutait,
En parlant du chemin de fer.

Tell me, who did compose this song? } 2
    It was just three ditch diggers.
While drinking at a cabaret,
The mistress overheard them say,
While talking of the new railway.

Et voilà tout
That's All I Want

This is a wagoner's song. In his 1910 book, *"Les chansons de metiers,"* ("Songs of Professions")
Paul Olivier had this to say about wagoners: "All the skill of a wagoner boils down to knowing
how to give his horse the habitual commands: *'dia!'*, which means *'left'*, and *'hu! hau!'* which
means 'right'. In possession of these elements which constitute the entire technique of the
profession, the wagoner can peacefully attend to his personal affairs, which consist principally
of quenching his thirst at all the wayside inns and have his voice and his whip resonate throughout
the entire neighborhood."

Pay - san, donn' moi ta fil - le, Et voi - là tout! Pay-
Give me your daugh - ter, farm - er, That's all I want! Give

san, donn' moi ta fil - le, Et voi - là tout! Don - ne - la - moi, Z'en t'y pri -
me your daugh - ter, farm - er, That's all I want! Give her to me, That's my in -

ant, Tu m'y ren - dras le coeur con - tent. Don - ne - la - moi, Z'en t'y pri -
tent, And you will make my heart con - tent. Give her to me, That's my in -

ant, Tu m'y ren - dras le coeur con - tent: Et voi - là tout!
tent, And you will make my heart con - tent: That's all I want!

46

Je m'en vais voir ma maîtresse
    Et voilà tout! } 2
Entre les onze heur's et minuit, } 2
A la fenêtre de son lit,
    Et voilà tout!
	I'm going to see my sweetheart,
	    That's all I want! } 2
	Between eleven and midnight, } 2
	Beneath her window I'll alight.
	    That's all I want!

- Dormez-vous, Jeann' ma mie?
    Et voilà tout! } 2
Si vous dormez, réveillez-vous.
C'est votre amant qui parle à vous. } 2
    Et voilà tout!
	"Say, Jeann' dear, are you sleeping?" } 2
	    That's all I want!
	"If you are sleeping - time to wake,
	Your lover's here, make no mistake." } 2
	    That's all I want!

- Je n'y dors, j'n'y sommeille. } 2
    Et voilà tout!
Toute la nuit, je pense à vous. } 2
Mon cher ami, marions-nous!
    Et voilà tout!
	"I'm up, I am not sleepy" } 2
	    That's all I want!
	"For all night long I think instead,
	My dearest love, it's time we wed." } 2
	    That's all I want!

Faut parler à mon père,
    Et voilà tout! } 2
A ma mère, à tous mes parents.
Pour moi, j'en ai le coeur content. } 2
    Et voilà tout!
	"You must go talk to father."
	    That's all I want! } 2
	"And to my mother and family,
	My heart is happy, don't you see?" } 2
	    That's all I want!

- Paysan, donn'-moi ta fille, } 2
    Et voilà tout!
Donne-la moi z'en t'y priant: } 2
Tu m'y rendras le coeur content
    Et voilà tout!
	"Give me your daughter, farmer." } 2
	    That's all I want!
	"Give her to me - that's my intent,
	And you will make my heart content." } 2
	    That's all I want!

- Ma fille est trop jeunette. } 2
    Et voilà tout!
Elle est trop jeune encor'd'un an: } 2
Faites l'amour en attendant.
    Et voilà tout!
	"My daughter is too young yet." } 2
	    That's all I want!
	She is too young to wed, I fear; } 2
	Court her for another year."
	    That's all I want!

- L'amour je n'veux plus faire. } 2
    Et voilà tout!
Garçon qui fait l'amour long-temps } 2
Risque fort à perdre son temps.
    Et voilà tout!
	"I do not care for courting." } 2
	    That's all I want!
	The boy who courts for a long time, } 2
	He strongly risks a waste of time."
	    That's all I want!

Le cordonnier qui se fait moine
The Shoemaker Who Made Himself a Monk

A traditional hatred existed between other journeymen and journeymen shoemakers. Whenever a journeyman encountered a shoemaker along the road, he never failed to cry out: *"Passe au large, sale puant!"* (Make way, dirty stinker!) - due, no doubt to the pungent odor of freshly tanned leather. They were also reputed to be drunkards. The story was told of a shoemaker who observed a drunk staggering past his shop on Thursday, and sadly saying to himself: "And that's how I'll be Sunday!"

J'suis cor - don - nier de mon mé - tier. J'suis cor - don - nier de mon mé -
A shoe-mak - er, yes, that is me. A shoe-mak - er, yes, that is

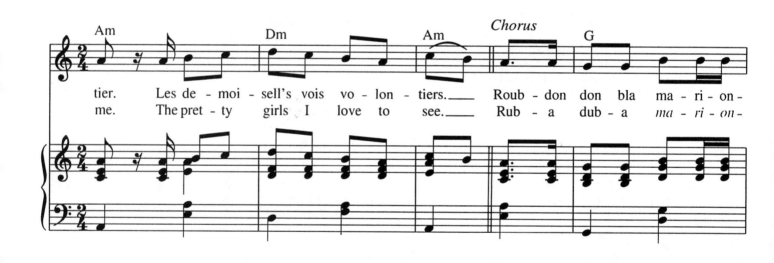

tier. Les de - moi - sell's vois vo - lon - tiers.___ Roub - don don bla ma - ri - on -
me. The pret - ty girls I love to see.___ Rub - a dub - a ma - ri - on -

Chorus

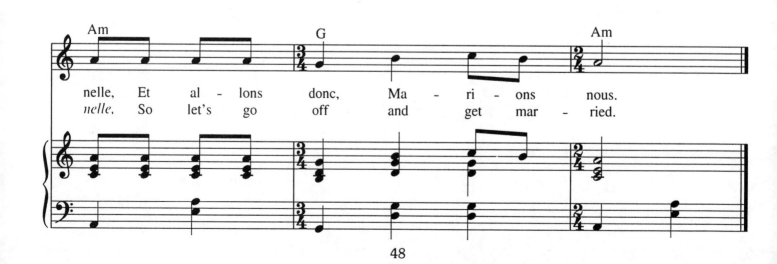

nelle, Et al - lons donc, Ma - ri - ons nous.
nelle, So let's go off and get mar - ried.

J'en aima une, j'en aima deux, (2)
L'un' de la vill', l'autr' du faubourg. *Chorus*

Cell' de la vill' j' ai demandé; (2)
Ses parents me l'ont refusée. *Chorus*

Du chagrin que j'en prenderai (2)
Pèr' capucin je m'y ferai. *Chorus*

Al'église j'y prêcherai.(2)
Tout en prêchant, j'y pleurerai. *Chorus*

Pour un' fille que j'ai d'mandée, (2)
Que ses parents m'ont refusée. *Chorus*

Tout l'mond' sera bien étonné (2)
D'y voir un capucin pleurer. *Chorus*

I did love one, I did love two, (2)
From city and from suburbs, too. *Chorus*

The city girl I courted so, (2)
Her parents then to me said no. *Chorus*

In sorrow I will leave my home, (2)
A Capuchin I will become. *Chorus*

A sermon I'll preach bye and bye, (2)
And while I'm preaching, I will cry. *Chorus*

All for a girl I wanted so, (2)
A girl whose parents did say no. *Chorus*

The people won't believe their ears, (2)
To see a Capuchin in tears. *Chorus*

Nous irons à Valparaiso
We're Bound for Valparaiso

The Chilean port of Valparaiso was a major port of call for 19th century French sailing ships. They sailed around the redoubtable Cape Horn, loaded down with cotton and silk goods, furniture and other manufactured products from Paris, to return charged with silver, tin, copper and leather. This song dates from 1811. Its *"Franglais"* refrains are typical of sea songs of the day.

Har-di les gars! vir' au guin-deau! Good-bye, fa-re well! good-bye, fa-re-well!
Let's go, my boys! the wind-lass, ho! Good-bye, fare ye well! good-bye, fare ye well!

Har-di les gars! a-dieu Bor-deaux Hour-ra, oh Mex-i-co-o-o-o! Au
Let's go, my boys. fare-well Bor-deaux Hur-rah, oh Mex-i-co-o-o-o! A-

Cap Horn il ne fe-ra pas chaud, Haul a-way! hé! Ou-la tcha-lez!
round Cape Horn there blows a cold gale, Haul a-way! hey! All haul a-way!

a fair la pêch' au ca-cha-lot, Hal' ma-te-lot! hé-ho, Hiss' hé ho!
we're fish-ing for the great sperm whale, Haul a way so! hey ho, Hoist, hey ho!

Plus d'un y laissera sa peau!   More than one lad will lose his life,
Good bye farewell! (2)   Goodbye, fare ye well, (2)
Adieu misèr' adieu bateau!   Farewell, the boat - farewell the strife,
Houra! oh Mexico!   Hurrah! Oh Mexico!
Ho! Ho! Ho!   Ho! Ho! Ho!
Et nous irons à Valparaiso!   And we are bound for Valparaiso!
Haul away!   Haul away!
Hé! Oula tchalez!   Hey! All haul away!
Où d'autr'y laisseront leurs os!   Where other bones will bleach ere we go!
Hal' matelot!   Haul away so!
Hé! Ho! Hiss'hé! Ho!   Hey! Ho! Hoist, hey ho!

Ceux qui r'viendront pavillon haut!   Those that return with flags on high,
Good bye farewell! (2)   Goodbye, fare ye well, (2)
C'est Premier Brin de matelot!   He's a real sailor - that's no lie!
Houra! oh Mexico!   Hurrah! Oh Mexico!
Ho! Ho! Ho!   Ho! Ho! Ho!
Pour la bordée ils seront à flot!   And for a spree, you can bet your life,
Haul away!   Haul away!
Hé! Oula tchalez!   Hey! All haul away!
Bons pour le rack, la fill', le couteau!   Good for the rack, the girl and the knife!
Hal' matelot!   Haul away so!
Hé! Ho! Hiss'hé! Ho!   Hey! Ho! Hoist, hey ho!

Le pont de Morlaix
The Morlaix Bridge

The bridge over the river cutting through Morlaix (in Finistère) was built at the end of the 19th century. The pedestrian walkway over the bridge was the favorite locale for sailers to "check out the action."

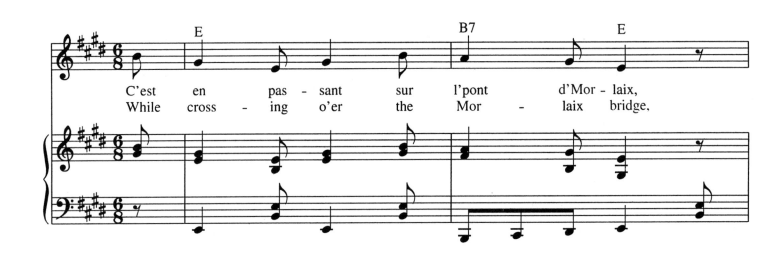

C'est en pas - sant sur l'pont d'Mor - laix,
While cross - ing o'er the Mor - laix bridge,

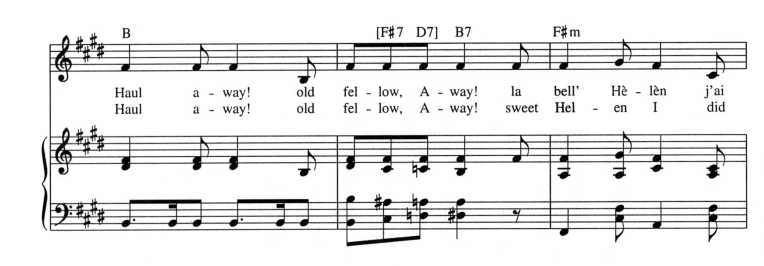

Haul a - way! old fel - low, A - way! la bell' Hè - lèn j'ai
Haul a - way! old fel - low, A - way! sweet Hel - en I did

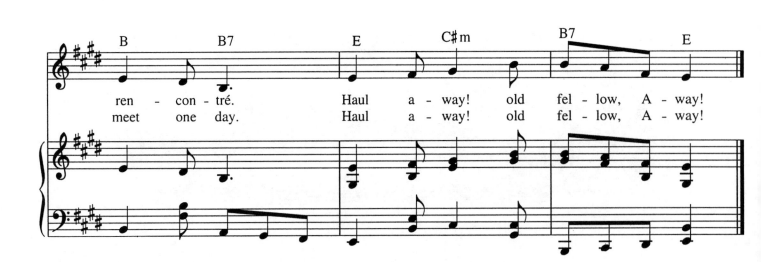

ren - con - tré. Haul a - way! old fel - low, A - way!
meet one day. Haul a - way! old fel - low, A - way!

Bien humblement j'lai saluée
Haul away!
Old fellow away!
D'un doux sourir' ell' m'a r'mercié,
Haul away!
Old fellow away!

Politely I did say good day,
Haul away!
Old fellow away!
With a sweet smile she turned my way,
Haul away!
Old fellow away!

Similarly

Mais j'ai bien vu qu'c'est charité,
Car c'est un' dam' de qualité

But I saw it was charity,
She was a woman of quality.

C'est la fill' d'un cap'tain nantais,
A matelot n'sera jamais.

The daughter of a Nantes captain,
Is never for a sailor man.

Pour nous sont les garces de quais,
Qui vol', qui mentent, qui font tuer.

The dockside whores give us a thrill,
They steal, they lie, they make us kill.

Je n'étal' plus, j'vas tout larguer,
J'vas fair' mon trou dans la salée.

I'm casting off - I'll make no bones,
I'm going down to Davy Jones.

Mat'lots, mon coeur est embrumé,
Buvons quand mêm' à sa beauté.

My boys, my heart is feeling low,
Let's drink to her before we go.

Encor' un coup pour étarquer,
Hiss' le grand foc, tout est payé.

Before we part just one more cup,
Hoist the mainsail, I'm all paid up.

Sont les fill's de La Rochelle
It's the Girls of La Rochelle

Sont les fill's de La Ro-chel-le, Ont ar-mé un bâti-
It's the girls of La Ro-chelle, Who have e-quipped a sail-ing

ment, Ont ar-mé un bâ-ti-ment, Pour al-ler fai-re la
ship, Have e-quipped a sail-ing ship, To sail off on a long

cour-se de-dans les mers du__ Le-vant. Ah! la feuil-le s'en-vo-le, s'en-
voy-age, To Le-vant they'll make__ the trip, Ah! the leaf, It flies off, It flies

vo-le. Ah! la feuil-le s'en-vo-le au vent!
ov-er. Ah! the leaf flies a-way in wind!

La grand'vergue est en ivoire,	The main yard is made of ivory,
Les poulies en diamant. (2)	And the pulleys are diamonds bright. (2)
La grand'voile est en dentelle,	The mainsail is made of lace,
La misaine en satin blanc.	And the foresail of satin white.
Les cordages du navire	And the rigging of the vessel,
Sont des fils d'or et d'argent. (2)	Gold and silver everywhere. (2)
Et la coque est en bois rouge,	While the hull is made of redwood,
Travaillé fort proprement.	Put together with great care.
L'équipage du navire,	The crew members of the vessel
C'est tout filles de quinze ans. (2)	Are all girls fifteen years old, (2)
Le cap'taine qui les commande,	And the captain who commands them,
Est le roi des bons enfants.	Is a king - handsome and bold.
Hier faisant sa promenade	Yesterday, taking a stroll
Dessus le gaillard d'avant, (2)	Along the deck before the mast, (2)
Aperçut une brunette,	He did spy a dark-haired maiden,
Qui pleurait dans les haubans.	And her tears were flowing fast.
"Qu'avez-vous, jeune brunette,	"What's the matter, young brunette,
Qu'avez-vous à pleurer tant? (2)	Why do you weep so bitterly? (2)
Av'vous perdu père et mère,	Have you lost father and mother,
Ou quelqu'un de vos parents."	Or someone you love dearly?"
"J'ai perdu la rose blanche,	"I did lose the pretty white rose,
Qui s'en fut la voil' au vent. (2)	Blown away in the stiff breeze. (2)
Elle est partie vent arrière,	It is gone - caught by a headwind,
Reviendra-z-en louvoyant.	Tack around, I beg you please."*

*Did he...? We'll never know.

Le trente et un du mois d'août
It Was on August Thirty-First

This song commemorates the engagement of August 31, 1800, in the course of which Captain Surcourf of the *Confiance*, captured the British man-of-war, *Kent*, which had a crew of 400 men and mounted 38 cannons.

Le trente et un du mois d'a - oût, Nous vîm's ve - nir sous l'vent à nous. Le trente et nous. U - ne fré - ga - te d'An - gle - ter - re, Qui fen - dait l'air et puis les flots, C'é - tait pour al - ler à Bor - deaux. U - ne fré - deaux.

It was on Aug - ust thir - ty first, We saw it, fast as it could go. It was on go. A Brit - ish fri - gate speed - ing our way, That cut through the air and the waves, It was a - head - ing for Bor - deaux. A Brit - ish deaux.

Chorus

Buvons un coup, buvons en deux, } 2
A la santé des amoureux,
A la santé du Roi de France,
Et merde pour le Roi d'Angleterre, }
Qui nous a déclaré la guerre. } 2

Le commandant du bâtiment }
Fit appeler son lieutenant } 2
-Lieutenant, te sens-tu capable
Dis-moi, te sens-tu assez fort
Pour prendre l'Anglais de plein bord? } 2 *Chorus*

Le lieutenant, fier z'et hardi }
Lui répondit: - Capitain', oui } 2
Faites branl'bas dans l'équipage,
Je vas z'hisser not' pavillon,
Qui rest'ra haut, nous le jurons. *Chorus* } 2

Le maître donne un coup d'sifflet }
Pour fair' monter les deux bordées. } 2
Tout est paré pour l'abordage
Hardis gabiers, fiers matelots, }
Brav's canonniers, mousses petiots. } 2 *Chorus*

Vir' lof pour lof, en arrivant, }
Je l'abordions par son avant, } 2
A coups de haches et de grenades,
De pieux, de sabr'z et mousquetons }
En trois cinq-sec je l'arrimions. } 2 *Chorus*

Que dira-t-on du grand raffiot, }
A Brest, à Londres et à Bordeaux } 2
Qu'a laissé prendr' son équipage
Par un corsair' de dix canons, }
Lui qu'en avait trente et si bons? } 2 *Chorus*

Chorus

Let's drink a cup, let us drink two, }
To the health of the lovers we knew. } 2
Let us drink to the king of France,
And to hell with the damned English king, }
Who upon us this war did bring. } 2

The commandant of the warship }
Called his lieutenant unto him. } 2
"Lieutenant, do you feel you're able,
Tell me, I ask you to decide,
To take the English by a broadside?" } 2 *Chorus*

The lieutenant, hardy and proud, }
Answered to him: "My captain, yes. } 2
Just clear the decks, summon the crew,
Our colors I will hoist on high; }
We swear to you, there they will fly. } 2 *Chorus*

The master blows his whistle then, }
To call the watches to their stations. } 2
The deck is cleared for the boarding
Topmen and sailors all are poised, }
Brave canoneers and cabin boys. } 2 *Chorus*

Veer to the side as we arrive, }
I will now board him at his prow. } 2
With hatchet blows and with grenades,
With musketoons and swords and stakes, }
In no time flat the ship we'll take. } 2 *Chorus*

What will the say of that big ship, }
In Brest, in London, or Bordeaux, } 2
That let itself be overcome
By a corsair with ten cannons - }
He who had thirty heavy guns? } 2 *Chorus*

57

Chère Elise
Dear Elise

This never-ending song dates from the early 19th century. With a different melody, it is virtually identical to the American song, "There's A Hole In The The Bucket".

A - vec quoi faut - il cher - cher l'eau,　Chère E - li - se,　Chère E -
With what shall I go get the wa - ter, Dear E - li - se,　Dear E -

li - se,　A - vec quoi faut - il cher - cher l'eau?　A - vec un
li - se,　With what shall I go get the wa - ter? Why, with a

seau,　Mon cher Eu - gè - ne,　Cher Eu - gè - ne, a - vec un seau.
pail,　My dear Eu - gene,_____ Dear-Eu gene, how a - bout a pail?

- Mais le seau, il est percé.
Chère Élise, chère Élise,
Mais le seau, il est percé.
-Faut le boucher, mon cher Eugène,
Cher Eugène, faut le boucher.

"But the pail, it has a hole,
Dear Elise, dear Elise,
But the pail it has a hole."
"Then plug it up, my dear Eugene,
Dear Eugene, then plug it up."

Similarly

-Avec quoi faut-il le boucher?
-Avec d'la paille, mon cher Eugène.

"But how shall I plug it up..."
"Just use some straw..."

-Mais la paille n'est pas coupée.
-Faut la couper, mon cher Eugène.

"But the straw - it isn't cut..."
"Then cut it down..."

-Avec quoi faut-il la couper?
-Avec une faux, mon cher Eugène.

"But with what should it be cut..."
"How 'bout a scythe..."

- Mais la faux n'est pas affûtée.
- Faut l'affûter, mon cher Eugène.

"But the scythe, it isn't sharp..."
"Then sharpen it..."

-Avec quoi faut-il l'affûter?
-Avec une pierre, mon cher Eugène.

"With what shall I sharpen it..."
"Perhaps a stone..."

- Mais la pierre n'est pas mouillée.
- Faut la mouiller, mon cher Eugène.

"But the stone, it isn't wet..."
"So wet it, then..."

-Avec quoi faut-il la mouiller?
-Avec de l'eau, mon cher Eugène.

"Tell me how should it be wet..."
"With H_2O..."

- Avec quoi faut - il chercher l'eau?...

"With what shall I get the water..."

...and so on...

59

Malbrough s'en va-t-en guerre
Malbrough is Off to Battle

It is September 11, 1709, near the hamlet of Malplaquet, in the north of France. On one side there is a force of 120,000 British and Dutch soldiers, and 120 cannons, under the command of Eugène de Savoie and John Churchill, the Duke of Marlborough. Opposing them are 80,000 French soldiers, led by Claude-Louis-Hector, *duc de Villars*, and Louis-François, *duc de Boufflers*. These two armies battle each other the whole day long to gain the supremacy of the north-west region of the kingdom of Louis XIV. The English win the day, and the fame of Churchill/Marlborough is assured. This song, which grew out of that battle, has absolutely nothing to do with reality. You may recognize the melody as, "For He's A Jolly Good Fellow."

Mal - brough s'en va-t - en guer - re, Mi - ron - ton, mi - ron-ton, mi - ron - tai - ne, Mal -
Mal - brough is off to bat - tle, Rit - tle - rat, rit - tle-rat, rit - tle rat - tle, Mal -

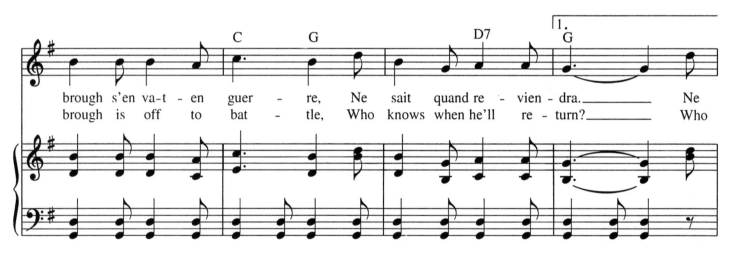

brough s'en va-t - en guer - re, Ne sait quand re - vien - dra._____ Ne
brough is off to bat - tle, Who knows when he'll re - turn?_____ Who

sait quand re - vien-dra,_____ Ne sait quand re - vien-dra._____ Il sez._____
knows when he'll re - turn?_____ who knows when he'll re - turn._____ He ough._____

Il reviendra-z-à Pâques,
Mironton, mironton, mirontaine,
Il reviendra-z-à Pâques,
Ou à la Trinité. (3)

He will return at Easter,
Rittle - rat, rittle - rat, rittle rattle,
He will return at Easter,
Or at the Trinity, (3)

Similarly

La Trinité se passe,
Malbrough ne revient pas. (3)

The Trinity is over...
Malbrough does not return. (3)

Madame à sa tour monte,
Si haut qu'elle peut monter. (3)

Madame climbs up her tower...
As high as she can go. (3)

Ell' voit venir son page,
Tout de noir habillé. (3)

She sees her page approaching...
He is all dressed in black. (3)

"Beau page, mon beau page,
Quelles nouvell's apportez?" (3)

"Dear page, my sweet, dear page...
What news do you bring me?" (3)

"Aux nouvell's que j'apporte,
Vos beaux yeux vont pleurer. (3)

"The news that I am bringing...
Will make your eyes weep tears." (3)

Quittez vos habits roses,
Et vos satins brochés. (3)

"Take off your rosy clothing...
And your satin brocade. (3)

Monsieur Malbrough est mort,
Est mort et enterré. (3)

"Monsieur Malbrough is dead...
He's dead and buried, too." (3)

J' l'ai vu porter en terre,
Par quatre-z-officiers.(3)

"I watched as he was carried...
By four brave officers." (3)

L'un portait sa cuirasse,
L'autre son bouclier. (3)

One man carried his breastplate...
The other had his shield." (3)

L'un portait son grand sabre,
L'autre ne portait rien. (3)

One carried his great sabre...
The other had nothing." (3)

A l'entour de sa tombe,
Romarin fut planté. (3)

And all around his tomb...
They planted rosemary." (3)

Sur la plus haute branche,
Un rossignol chantait. (3)

"And on the highest branch, then...
A nightingale did sing." (3)

On vit voler son âme,
Au travers des lauriers. (3)

"We saw his soul go flying
Through laurels it did go." (3)

La cérémonie faite,
Chacun s'en fut coucher. (3)

"The ceremony over...
Each one went off to bed.(3)

Les uns avec leurs femmes,
Et les autres tout seuls! (3)

"Some went to bed with their wives...
And others all alone. (3)

J' n'en dis pas davantage,
Car en voilà-z-assez" (1)

"There's nothing more to tell you...
I think I've said enough." (1)

Changement de garnison
Changing the Garrison

Pleu - rez, pleu -
O, weep, o,

rez, bel - les des Mai-sons-Neu - ves, Pleu - rez, pleu - rez, bel -
weep, You girls of Mai-sons-Neu - ves, O, weep, O, weep, you

les de Sain - te - Croix. Jus - qu'à ce soir il vous faut res - ter
girls of Sain - te - Croix. Un - til to night you have to re - main

veu - ves, Et dans cha - que mai - son chan - ger de gar - ni - son.
wid - ows, And in each house and home, A change of gar - ris - son.

Belles aussi d'Aramits et d'Arette,
 Belles d'Accous,
 Lescoun, Ousse et Védous,
Pleurez celui que votre coeur regrette,
 Et dans un seul moment
 Vous faut changer d'amant.

A vos amants faites bien la conduite,
 Et par la main,
 Jusqu'a moitié chemin;
A la grand' halte il vous faudra de suite,
 Pour changer de vallon,
 Changer de bataillon.

Belles d'en haut, regrettez moins les vôtres;
 Belles d'en bas,
 Ne vous tourmentez pas;
De ces amants les uns valent les autres:
 Si les premiers sont beaux,
 Les autres sont nouveaux.

Chez vous, beautés qu'un beau sapeur astique
 Toujours, dit-on.
 L'amour est de planton.
Pour la constance, vive la musique,
 Longtemps on est d'accord.
 Vive l'état-major!

A vos amants ne soyez point rebelles;
 Pour ces lurons,
 Nous vous épouserons.
Pourvu pourtant que vous restiez fidèles
 Bien vertueusement
 A ce seul régiment.

Nous donnerons, pour soutenir la France,
 Postérité
 De bonne qualité;
Nos fils naîtront le nez rouge garance,
 Numéro neuf au front;
 A ça n'y a pas d'affront.

Also you girls of Aramits and Arette,
 Girls of Accous,
 Lescoun, Ousse and Védous,
Weep for the one for whom your heart is breaking,
 In the twinkling of an eye,
 Your new lover will come by.

As for your lovers, you must say goodbye now,
 And by the hand,
 Lead them just half the way;
And when they halt, you have no time to cry now,
 The old ones march away,
 The new arrive today.

Girls from the heights, do not pine for your lovers,
 Girls from below,
 Don't torment yourselves so;
For your boyfriends - the ones are like the others,
 If the first are true,
 The other ones are new.

Now, all you girls, may you all have brave soldiers,
 For, as they say,
 True love is on the way.
As for constancy - just let the music play,
 For we all do agree:
 Long live the brave army!

Do not rebel against your soldier sweethearts,
 And for these guys,
 We'll make you all their wives.
But that will only be if you remain all faithful,
 And keep yourselves content
 With just this regiment.

And we will give, that France might be defended,
 Posterity
 Of the best quality;
Our sons will be born with noses of a bright red,[1]
 And sporting "number nine,"[2]
 Which is just mighty fine.

---

1. The color of the uniform trousers in 1914.
2. Evidently the number of the regiment.

LE CHANGEMENT DE GARNISON

OUS ÉTIONS DIX FILLES DANS UN PRÉ

Nous étions dix fill's dans un pré,
Tout's les dix à marier :
Y avoit Dine,
Y avoit Chine,
Y avoit Claudine et Martine ;
Ah ! ah !
Cath'rinette et Cath'rina,
Y avoit la belle Suzon,
La duchess' de Montbazon ;
Y avoit Madelaine,
Il y avoit la du Maine.

Nous étions dix filles dans un pré
We Were Ten Girls in a Lea

Nous é - tions dix fill's dans un pré, Tout's les dix a - ma - ri - er Y'a - voit
We were ten young girls in a lea, All the ten would mar - ried be. There was

Di - ne, Y'a - voit Chi - ne, Y'a - voit Clau - dine et Mar - ti - ne. Ah! ah! Cath - ri - nette et
Di - ne, There was Chi - ne, There was Clau - dine and Mar - tin - ne. Ah! ah! Cath - ri nette and

Cath' - ri - na, Y'a - voit la bel - le Su - zon, La du - chess' de Mont - ba - zon,
Cath' - ri - na, There was the pret - ty Su - zon, The du - chess of Mont - ba - zon,

Y'a - voit Ma - de - lei - ne, Il y'a - voit la du Mai - ne.
There was Ma - de - lei - ne, And there was *la du Mai* - *ne.*

Le fils du roi vint à passer,
  L'fils du roi vint à passer,
    Salua Dine,
    Salua Chine;
  Salua Claudine et Martine,
    Ah! ah!
  Cath'rinette et Cath'rina;
  Salua la belle Suzon,
  La duchess' de Montbazon,
    Salua Madeleine,
  Embrassa la du Maine.

A toutes il fit un cadeau,
  A tout's il fit un cadeau:
    Bague à Dine,
    Bague à Chine;
  Bague à Claudine et Martine,
    Ah! ah!
  Cath'rinette et Cath'rina;
  Bague à la belle Suzon,
  La duchess' de Montbazon,
    Bague à Madeleine,
  Diamants à la du Maine.

Puis il leur offrit à coucher,
  Il leur offrit à coucher:
    Paille à Dine,
    Paille à Chine,
  Paille à Claudine et Martine,
    Ah! ah!
  Cath'rinette et Cath'rina;
  Paille à la belle Suzon,
  La duchess' de Montbazon,
    Paille à Madeleine,
  Beau lit à la du Maine.

Puis toutes il les renvoya,
  Toutes il les renvoya:
    Chassa Dine,
    Chassa Chine,
  Chassa Claudine et Martine,
    Ah! ah!
  Cath'rinette et Cath'rina;
  Chassa la belle Suzon,
  La duchess' de Montbazon,
    Chassa Madeleine,
  Et garda la du Maine.

The king's own son went passing by,
  The king's son went passing by.
    Greeted Dine,
    Greeted Chine;
  Greeted Claudine and Martine,
    Ah! ah!
  Cath'rinette and Cathrina;
  Greeted the pretty Suzon,
  The Duchess of Montbazon,
    Greeted Madeleine
  And embraced *la du Maine.*

To each of them he gave a gift,
  To each one he gave a gift:
    Ring to Dine,
    Ring to Chine,
  Ring to Claudine and Martine,
    Ah! ah!
  Cath'rinette and Cathrina;
  Ring to the pretty Suzon,
  The Duchess of Montbazon,
    Ring to Madeleine,
  And diamonds to *la du Maine.*

He offered then to lodge them all,
  He offered to lodge them all:
    Straw for Dine,
    Straw for Chine,
  Straw for Claudine and Martine,
    Ah! ah!
  Cath'rinette and Cathrina;
  Straw for the pretty Suzon,
  The Duchess of Montbazon,
    Straw for Madeleine,
  Nice bed for *la du Maine.*

And then he sent them all away,
  Then he sent them all away,
    Kicked out Dine,
    Kicked out Chine,
  Kicked out Claudine and Martine,
    Ah! ah!
  Cath'rinette and Cathrina;
  Kicked out the pretty Suzon,
  The Duchess of Montbazon,
    Kicked out Madeleine,
  But he kept *la du Maine.*

Départ pour le tour de France
Departure for the "Tour de France"

This *tour de France* has nothing to do with the modern French bicycle race in which the cyclists pedal through the French countryside and up and down the Alps for two weeks each year. It is rooted in a much earlier tradition: *compagnonnage* (journeymen), which dates from the 12th century. *Compagnonnage* grew out of opposition to the all-powerful guilds, which all too rarely admitted journeymen workers into their associations. Forced to look beyond the guilds for employment, these journeymen took to the open road; the *tour de France* was the first of their obligations. For long years they scattered their jolly songs and good humor along the grand routes of France. They adopted colorful nicknames, based on their city or region of origin, coupled with a fanciful appellation: *Mâconnais l'âme des Arts* ("...the soul of the Arts"), *Montpellier la lyre d'amour* ("...the lyre of love"), *Dauphiné prêt à bien faire* ("...ready to do well").

Partons, chers com-pa-gnons, Le de-voir nous l'or-don-ne; Voi-
Com-pan-ions, Let's be off, Our du-ty gives the or-der; The

ci le vrai mo-ment qu'il faut bat-tre aux champs.
mo-ment has ar-rived that we must take to the road.

L'hi-ver est é-cou-lé, La neige et la froi-du-re;
Win-ter now is a-way, Snow and the freez-ing weath-er;

On voit dès à présent revenir le printemps.

And we see from now on, spring-time has come again.

Le sac dessus le dos, On m'y fait la conduite Le long de mon chemin, Mais marchant le grand' train. L'on entend les oiseaux Qui dis'nt dans leur langage: - Oh! qu'i' y a du plaisir D'les entendre partir.	The sack is on my back, And I am on my way now. I'm off down my long road, But walking with great strides. I can hear the birds, Who say in their language: "O! what a happy day, To hear them go on their way."
Y allons fair' nos adieux A nos joli's maîtresses. Après nous leur dirons: C'est demain qu'nous partons. - Cher amant, tu t'en vas! Oh! tu m'y laiss's, tu m'abandonnes Enceinte d'un enfant. Mon p'tit coeur s'en va mourant.	Let's go say our goodbyes To our pretty sweethearts; Then we will say to them That tomorrow we're gone. "Dear heart, can you leave? You leave me here - I'm abandoned, Pregnant with a child. My heart will surely break."
- Ne dites rien, ma mie, R'console-toi, ma blonde! Je reviendrai z'un jour Accomplir nos amours. - Mais tu t'en vas là-bas, Au vers des autres blondes. Un' fixera ton choix... Tu n'penseras plus à moi!	"Say nothing, my love. Console yourself, my fair one. I'll come back one day To satisfy our love." "You're going far away, You will meet other fair ones. One will catch your eye — You never will think of me."

Les filles d'Avignon
The Girls of Avignon

Les filles d'Avignon
Sont comme des melons,) 2
Sur cent cinquante,
N'y' en a pas de mûr;
La plus charmante
N'a pas le cœur bien sûr.
    Laire, laire, lan la lan laire,
    Lan laire, laire landerira. *Chorus*

The girls of Avignon,
They are just like melons.) 2
Out one hundred fifty,
A ripe one is not around;
The most attractive -
Her heart cannot be found.
    Laire, laire, lan la lan laire,
    Lan laire, laire landerira. *Chorus*

La guitare
The Guitar

André-Joseph Exaudet (1710 - 1762) wrote his famous minuet in 1758. Thirty years later, having in the meantime become a "standard," Lévier de Champ-Rion set his delightful poem in praise of the guitar to its familiar strains.

Words by Levrier de Champ - Rion
Music : Minuet by Exaudet

Un char-mant in - stru-ment qui pré - pa - re
Ex - er - cez, Con - nais-sez vo - tre man - che.
A pleas-ant in - stru-ment that makes read - y
While you play ev' - ry day, Keep your wrist high,

aux coeurs ten - dres des plai - sirs, Ré-pond à leurs sou - pirs, N'est - ce pas la gui - tar - re.
Trip-lez vos ar - pe - gi - os dans un jeu tout nou - veau, Que vo - tre âme s'é - pan - che.
ten - der hearts for plea-sure, Gives them a full meas-ure, Of course, If is the gui - tar.
Tri - ple your ar - peg - gio, That is the way to go, And may your soul just pour forth.

A sa - voir E - mou-voir; elle ex - cel - le.
De vos doigts, A la voix, Nul di - vor - ce.
It can touch Ve - ry much, None does bet - ter.
Fin - ger - tips To your lips, No di - vorce.

Le grand projet
The Grand Project

The "grand project" of Marie Jean Antoine Nicolas de Caritat, marquis de Condorcet (1743-1794), philosopher, mathematician and revolutionary, was nothing but the Republican itself. It was he who, after the attempt flight in favor of a republic. He was the most influential member of the committee charged with drafting the new constitution, which was presented to the Convention on February 15, 1793. It was during this time that the trial of Louis XVI was taking place. Condorcet voted the king guilty of conspiring against the Republic. For a year he eluded arrest, finally falling victim to the Terror, when he was taken prisoner on April 7th, 1794. The next morning he was found dead in his cell.

ré. U - ne pu, pu, pu, U - ne ré, u - ne pu, U - ne ré - pu -
re, A___ pu, pu, pu, A___ re, a___ pu, A new re - pu -

bli - que bien dé - mo - cra - ti - que.
blic, That will be de - mo - cra - tic.

On porte aux cieux un héros
Tant qu'il est utile;
On jouit de ses travaux,
Ensuite on l'exile;
Cela n'est pas trop décent,
Mais c'est l'usage pourtant
    D'une ré, ré, ré,
    D'une pu, pu, pu,
        D'une ré,
        D'une pu,
    D'une république
    Bien démocratique.

We lift skyward a hero,
As long as he does serve us;
But ere long he has to go,
He does not deserve us.
That is not the way to be,
But it is the way, you see,
    Of a re, re, re,
    Of a pu, pu, pu,
        Of a re,
        Of a pu,
    Of a good republic,
    That is democratic.

Sans craindre d'un importun
Les discours infâmes,
Nous mettrons tout en commun
Jusques à nos femmes.
Si nous agissons ainsi,
C'est pour mieux saisir l'esprit
    D'une ré, ré, ré,
    D'une pu, pu, pu,
        D'une ré,
        D'une pu,
    D'une république
    Bien démocratique.

Without fearing anyone,
Who may speak with venom,
We lump together everyone,
Even our women.
And if we react like this,
We're sure naught will go amiss,
    In a re, re, re,
    In a pu, pu, pu,
        In a re,
        In a pu,
    In our new republic,
    That is democratic.

Le franc républicain
The Frank Republican

"By a citizen who has always believed and still believes that what French liberty needs in order to generate popular support, is to strip off completely the bloody tunic which some ferocious men have donned, and to put on as quickly as possible an anglo-american suit."

So wrote the anonymous composer to this pre-Gilbert-and-Sullivan patter song in May 1795. It was during the period of massacres, assasinations and riots, that these clever appeal for sanity was written. The terms scattered throughout the song would have been well-known to contemporary listeners. Rather than trying to define and explain them all here (which would take several pages), I suggest browsing through a good encyclopedia.

Lors-que le froid jan-sé-nis-te nar-guait le chaud mo-li-nis-te pour ces
When the chil-ly Jan-se-nist in-sults the fier-y Mo-li-nist, For both these

deux par-tis en lis-te j'a-vais un é-gal dé-dain. Phi-lo-
part-ies, I in-sist, I have the ut-most of dis-dain. Ph'lo-so-

sophe et qui-é-tis-te, J'ab-ho-re le ter-ro-ris-te ja-co-
pher and qui-et-ist, I do ab-hor the ter-ror-ist, The Ja-co-

bin ou roy - a - lis - te, Et je suis ré - pub - li - cain.
bin or roy - al - ist, For I am a re - pub - li - cain.

Malgré R*** le sophiste,	Spite of R[1] ...the well-known sophist,
Malgré R*** le casuiste,	And of M[2] ...who is a casuist,
Et malgré tel journaliste,	And a certain journalist,
Caméléon écrivain,	Who's like a chameleon,
Je ne suis point capétiste,	I am not a Capétist,
Je ne suis point sorboniste,	And I am not a Sorbonist,
Je ne suis point anarchiste,	I am not an anarchist,
Je suis franc républicain.	I'm a frank republican.
Mon grand-père est Fayétiste,	My grandfather's Fayétist,
Ma grand-mère est alarmiste,	My grandmother's an alarmist,
Mon grand frère apologiste	Big brother's an apologist,
De la guerre et du tocsin;	All for the war and the tocsin.
Mais mon père est optimiste,	But my dad's an optimist,
Ma mère est tolérantiste,	Mama she's a tolerantist,
Aussi peu controversiste,	As well as a controversist -
Moi, je suis républicain.	But me, I'm a republican.
Mais comment, né monarchiste,	How can you, born monarchist,
Etes-vous panégyriste	Also be a panegyrist
D'un système antagoniste	For a system antagonist-ic,
Où le peuple est souverain?	Where people are sovereign?
Quand le plus grand nombre insiste	When the greatest number insist
Pour que ce régime existe	That this regime just must exist,
L'autre nombre à tort résiste;	The others wrongfully resist;
Et je suis républicain.	And I am a republican.
Mais il faut être papiste,	But one must be a Papist,
Seriez-vous donc calviniste,	Or could you be a Calvinist,
Talmudiste, ou koraniste?	A Talmudist or Koranist?
Qui, moi? J'aime mon prochain:	Me? I love my fellow man:
Lorsque avec peine il subsiste,	When with hardship he subsists,
Tant que je peux, je l'assiste;	I try my hardest to assist,
C'est en ce point que consiste	And in this very point consists
Le dogme républicain.	The true dogma republican.
Vienne enfin la paix, Ariste,	When peace comes at last, Ariste,
Chacun deviendra théiste,	We will all become theist,
Jusqu'au matérialiste;	Or, perhaps, materialist,
Turc ou juif, grec ou romain,	Turk or Jew, Greek or Roman.
Le bonze aura l'air bien triste	The Bonze surely will be pissed,
Sur son trône d'améthyste	Upon his throne of amethyst,
Ebranlé par la baliste	But he never will be missed,
Du bon sens républicain.	By any good republican.

1. Robespierre (?)
2. Marat (?)

La danse française
The French Dance

January 12th, 1798, Bonaparte announces to the *Directoire* his plan for the invasion of England. The news traveled quickly, because this song appeared on that very date. Double meanings abound throughout the piece; *"L'allemande vient de finir"* is an allusion to the signature of the peace treaty of Campoformio (October, 1797) between France and Austria; "allemande" (which means "German") is well-known to square dancers, as in the call, "allemande left." Other allusions are explained below.

The projected invasion never took place because Bonaparte soon realized that the French navy did not "rule the waves." He turned his attention to his Egyptian campaign—but that's another story.

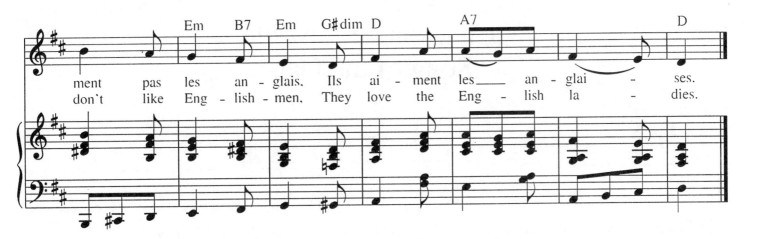

ment   pas   les   an - glais,   Ils   ai - ment   les___ an - glai - ses.
don't   like   Eng - lish - men,   They   love   the   Eng - lish la - dies.

Le Français donnera le bal,
    Il sera magnifique:
L'Anglais fournira le local,
    Et paiera la musique.
Nous, sur le refrain des couplets
    De nos rondes françaises,
Nous ferons chanter les Français
    Et danser les Anglaises.

D'abord par le Pas-de-Calais
    On doit entrer en danse;
Le son des instruments français
    Marquera la cadence:
Et comme l'Anglais ne saura
    Que danser les anglaises,
Bonaparte lui montrera
    Les figures françaises.

Dans nos entrechats, cette fois,
    Pour être plus à l'aise,
Laissons leurs casimirs étroits,
    Quittons la mode anglaise.
Portant cocardes et mousquets,
    Au lieu de ces fadaises,
Nous ferons goûter aux Anglais
    Les parures françaises.

Allons, mes amis, le grand rond,
    En avant, face-à-face:
Français, là-bas restez d'aplomb;
    Anglais, changez de place;
Vous, Monsieur Pitt, un balancé;
    Suivez la chaîne anglaise;
Pas de côté, croisé, chassé...
    C'est la danse française.

The French, they will present the ball,
    It will be somthing "hyper".
The English will supply the hall,
    And they will pay the piper.
While we, in playing the refrain
    Of our jolly chorus,
We'll make the French sing without pain,
    The British dance before us.

So first by the Pas-de-Calais,[1]
    Each on his partner with him,
The instruments of France will play,
    To keep us all in rhythm.
And since the Englishmen just know
    The steps of English dances,
Then Bonaparte will gladly show
    Just what the dance of France is.

And in our *entrechats*[2] this time,
    In order to jump better,
We'll leave the English style behind,
    Take off their cashmere sweater
We'll carry muskets and cockades,
    These trifles really tire.
We'll give the English a parade
    Of our French attire.

Come on, my friends, and circle right,
    And forward, face-to-face now;
The French, right there, remain upright,
    The English change your place now.
You, Mister Pitt,[3] now balance all,
    Grand right-and-left, you prance now;
Step to the side, across the hall,
    And that is the French dance now.

---

1. A play on words: Pas-de-Calais is the
    French department touching the Strait
    of Dover (nearest to England); *pas* means
    step - in this case, a dance step.
2. A common term in ballet - an athletic leap.
3. William Pitt, British Prime Minister
    at the time.

Chanson de l'aveine
Song of the Oats

mè - ne. A - veine, a - veine, a - vein - e, Que le beau temps t'a - mè - ne.
dai - ly. A - plant - ing oats so gai - ly, May we have good wea - ther dai - ly.

Voulez-vous savoir comment, comment, 　　On coupe l'aveine? Mon père la coupait ainsi: Puis se reposait à demi. *Chorus*	Would you really like to know, to know 　　How our oats are cut down? My father cut them down like this: Then he would take a little rest. *Chorus*
Voulez-vous savoir comment, comment, 　　On mange l'aveine? Mon père la mangeait ainsi: Puis se reposait à demi. *Chorus*	Would you really like to know, to know 　　How are oats are eaten? My father ate his oats like this: Then he would take a little rest *Chorus*

CHANSON DE L'AVEINE

Voulez-vous savoir comment, comment
On sème l'aveine ?
Mon père la semait ainsi :
Puis se reposait à demi,
Frappe du pied, puis de la main,
Un petit tour pour son voisin !
Aveine, aveine, aveine,
Que le beau temps t'amène. } (bis.)

Le petit matelot
The Little Sailor

This sailors' song dates from the 18th century, the period of great exploration and navigation of the Indian Ocean. It ends with the popular folkloric evocation of the story of Jonah and the whale.

C'é-tait un pe - tit ma-te - lot, Sur les flots de la mer in-dienn', C'é-tait un pe - tit ma-te - lot, Oh!__ oh!__ pe-tit ma - te - lot.

A lit-tle sail - or sailed a - way, On the waves of the In - di - an Sea. A lit-tle sail - or sailed a - way, Oh!__ oh!__ sailed a - way one day.

Voguait de Brest à Frisco.	Traveling Brest - San Francisco,
Sur les flots de la mer indienne.	On the waves of the Indian Sea,
Voguait de Brest à Frisco.	Traveling Brest - San Francisco,
Oh, oh, petit matelot.	Oh, oh, sailed away one day.

Similarly

Un jour le temps se fit très gros...	One day the weather, it turned bad...
Serr'les voil' tout le monde en haut...	Reef in the sails - everyone up...
Tombe de plus de vingt mètres de haut...	He fell from twenty meters high...
On mit la chaloupe à l'eau...	They put the sloop down on the sea...
Pour vite le tirer des flots...	To pull him out of the water...
Mais on ne sauva que son chapeau...	But they could save only his hat...
Sa vieille pipe et ses sabots...	His old pipe and his wooden shoes...
Peut-être bien que le p'tit matelot...	Maybe the little sailor man...
Est dans le ventre d'un cachalot...	Is in the belly of a whale...